D1088840

life in the peace zone

an american company town

Hugh Wilkerson and
John van der Zee

Collier Books
New York, New York

Copyright © 1971 by Hugh Wilkerson
Copyright © 1971 by John van der Zee

Designed by Joan Stoliar

All rights reserved. No part of this book
may be reproduced or transmitted in any
form or by any means, electronic or
mechanical, including photocopying,
recording or by any information storage and
retrieval system, without permission in
writing from the Publisher.

The Macmillan Company
866 Third Avenue, New York, N.Y. 10022
Collier-Macmillan Canada Ltd.,
Toronto, Ontario

Life in the Peace Zone is also published in a
hardcover edition by
The Macmillan Company.

Library of Congress Catalog Card Number: 70-156845

First Collier Books Edition 1971

Printed in the United States of America

You enter the tunnel about five hours north of San Francisco, after more than fifty miles of thickening redwood forest, shrinking neon, and growing darkness and gloom.

Now trees without tops—three-hundred-foot giants—crowd down to the roadside. The sun disappears, the surface of the road turns wet. In the stillness, strange, ancestral images—of lost children, beasts, cult-worship—begin playing about the edges of your mind. You begin to sense only the thinnest skin of contemporary man and his times covering a deep, primitive past.

Fifteen minutes later, back on the main highway, still in flickering light and shadow, surrounded by hillsides deep and dark with trees, you are suddenly thrown back into daylight, and there is an enormous gap in the forest; all along one side of the highway is a small city of mills, smokestacks and clustered look-alike houses, a town made of lumber, taking in logs, churning out neat stacks of siding, beams and two-by-fours like an industrial Williamsburg, a historical reconstruction of a company town. The immediate reaction is intense, emotional, and mixed: Here are the timber beasts, gnawing at the heart of the redwood forest; but here, too, is something else, perhaps more valuable than redwoods: a living American past of a kind being desperately fabricated in the Frontier This and Pioneer Thats springing up all over the West, and pursued at another level in the communes, forming, failing, regrouping, in rural and primitive areas all over America.

But this community—Scotia, California—is authentic, a true frontier creation, half-necessity, half-dream, an entire town dependent on a single firm for its existence, streets, homes, stores, gardens, school, bank, gym, post office, library—all the appendages of one lumber company's mills.

the mills

On a cold summer morning under a sky the color of cement, the town presents a tableau out of the first Industrial Revolution. Leaving the modest, look-alike houses grouped on either side of the ten-acre millpond where giant logs float half-submerged like dozing whales, the men come on their way to the mills, walking along the wet streets quickly, alone or in twos, a few riding bicycles, some carrying lunch buckets, newspapers, a thermos, others maneuvering cars or pickup trucks in competition with men driving in from outside for position in the dusty parking areas. Beside the pond, a company switch engine pulls a long line of flatcars loaded with logs just in from the woods toward an overhead crane with an enormous set of tongs, while from within the three mills, each the acreage of a small farm under roof, come the thump and clang of huge, complicated machinery being fine-tuned for the massive, precise work of turning logs into lumber. Finally, above it all, above the railyards and floating logs, over the growing mill noise and the quiet, tidy military-post-like residential streets, reaching out toward the mile upon mile of redwoods fringing the sky in every direction, come the ancient white plume and hoarse hoot of the factory whistle on the roof of Mill A. Another workday at Scotia begins.

Up close, the machinery of a redwood mill is terrifying in its size, force, and noise. Seventy-ton sections of log collide with the heavy momentum of freight cars. Exposed saw blades chew the air in endless rectangles, circles, rows. Whistles go off ten feet from your ear. Huge boilers give off heat that raises your sweat. On elevated rollers, sections of wood speed by on the journey from log to lumber, while on the floor, conveyor chains veer off at angles toward other parts of the mill. At every station there are things to trip over and get caught in; not only the machines, but even parts of them, levers, blades, arms, hooks, are large enough to maim or kill.

Standing in this tremendous concentration of noise and energy, watching men tend and operate the machines, you start to speak, and realize that the mill has struck you mute. Looking around, you recognize men on the line, standing like yourself, sealed off by the noise of the machines, suspended in a state of half willful deafness, half constant mechanical alert. Conversation is impossible, communication limited to minimal hand signals and nods; though the mill has a crew of perhaps sixty or seventy men, each man is, in reality, alone with the noise and the line.

17

In a corner of the huge hangar-like building, a twenty-foot length of glistening, barkless run. Everything in sight—chain, levers, gears, some of the most powerful mill machinery in the world. Just above the log, in a raised, windowed booth, sawyer Richard Moore, swinging levers with both hands, tumbles, rolls and flips the log into position on a heavy carriage, analyzing and deciding in seconds where he will make his first cut. Ahead, the band saw gleams sharply on its continuous run. Everything in sight—chain, levers, gears, saw—is built to giant scale, and moves with a giant's blunt, irrevocable motions.

As sawyer, Moore must, in seconds, appraise each log's grain and decide what sections, cut thick, will be sent on to the gang saw for siding and what, cut thin, will be edged and trimmed into beams, studs, strips and panelling. There are no second chances.

"The sawyer is the man," says a mill production superintendent.

Moore has spent three years learning his job, three years in which each log-loading was different, where a single error could ruin a saw, destroy a thousand board feet of prime heartwood, or let automatic machinery run wild. Often, his legs, back, shoulders, even his eyes have ached with the strain of concentration, and he recalls "wicked dreams"

18

of loose logs and flying lumber coming at him, nightmares so intense they woke him. As if in reaction to the noise and force around him, Moore has developed an on-the-job posture of stoic, almost expressionless calm. Methodically, without waste motion, he moves the truck-sized headrig coolly forward, and the saw screams into the log, shaving off a two-inch-wide cut like the first slice from a turkey. Now the headrig recoils back. With a huge crash and thump and great gasps of steam, the log is turned, tilted, prepared to be rolled forward again. Moore is ready for the second of the several hundred money-cuts he'll make today.

Following the hand signals of the production superintendent, you walk down the line, stepping over moving chains, waiting as at a streetcorner for a break in the passing chunks of wood so you can cross a row of rollers. You begin to notice the division of labor in the mill: most of the men merely tend the machines, feeding lumber in or taking it off; only a few men operate them. The same motions are repeated, and the pace rarely changes. In five minutes you see as much variety as most men who work on the line do in twenty years. There is a strong undercurrent of violence in an atmosphere of order, of force amid tranquility.

21

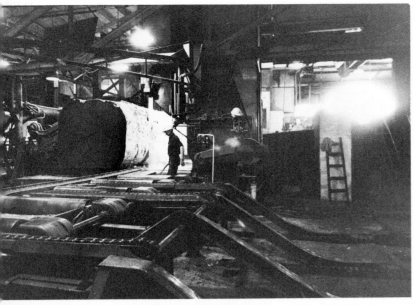

31

At an electronic console, below a row of wires or cords thrown in a shadow pattern on the wood by bright overhead light, a man stands operating a machine that edges slabs of wood from the headrig into recognizable lengths of lumber. The production superintendent taps the man on the arm and points to a relief man. Nodding, the edgerman leaves the line and follows his foreman across the floor to a large booth with a desk and chairs: the superintendent's office. Not until the door is closed can you be introduced.

The edgerman's name is Ernest De Marzi, and he lives near the town of Ferndale, a pastoral community of antique shops and old houses that calls itself "The Victorian Village."

De Marzi lives alone on a ranch where he runs a small herd of white-faced cattle, which he hopes to expand into a full-time beef and dairy operation. His ranch house furnishings—cow's skull, TV set, table, some farm magazines, a few clothes, boots—are hermit-like; the care goes into the herd. Every morning, De Marzi gets up at five o'clock, works for an hour or two cleaning the barn or mending fence, goes off to work in the mill, then puts in another couple of hours ranching when he returns in the evening. Asked if it's much of a shock to come from the quiet of his ranch into the noise and production pressure of the mill, De Marzi smiles and shakes his head in recognition. Is it ever. Like Richard Moore, he has had nightmares about his job, and he works with a similar air of rigid-faced competence.

De Marzi intends to take an early pension and retire to his ranch at fifty-five.

"I can't see these guys who slave in the mill for forty years until they get that pension at sixty-five. They'll be lucky to make it till sixty-seven, much less seventy or seventy-five. You just can't work like that and last forever."

35

Walking back onto the floor, the noise of the mill battering your ears and De Marzi's words on your mind, you begin to understand the necessity of a man's having a mental image of himself farming, fishing or travelling around the country in a camper after his days on the line are over, a means of distracting his sensibilities from the work while sustaining his attention to it. A personal end to the unending flow of lumber. A life to go to when the last whistle blows at the end of the last working day.

Looking around at the machinery, feeling the enormity of the noise and the silence of the men, you begin to realize that you could, just as well, right now be in Pittsburgh or Manchester or Essen as in a remote corner of Northern California, surrounded by redwood forest. Staring at the huge, complex system of belts, cranes, rollers, pulleys, saws, chains, consoles, hooks, gears, flywheels and levers, imagining two other mills this size plus the people and power it takes to operate them, and the length of time—more than a hundred years—that the company has been in business, you begin to wonder: How on earth did it all get here?

37

In the beginning, which in Scotia was about 1869, the town was a geographical fly-speck known as Forestville, in a corner of California with a corrugated topography, broad, swift rivers, and forests so dense early explorers found them impossible to walk through. For decades, the ruggedness of the country, combined with the sheer size of the redwoods and the general ignorance of their commercial qualities, was enough to discourage large-scale attempts at logging. But by the late 1860's, the woods of Maine and Michigan had been logged out and the smaller stands of redwood in California counties to the south were all but gone, so the men and the money came here, timber money, mining money, railroad money, money to buy land and lay track and import experienced lumberjacks and millhands from the old timberlands of the east and north. Especially from the Canadian province of New Brunswick. Once part of what the British named Nova Scotia, transplanted with Scots, New Brunswick offered a foretaste of Humboldt County, a maritime province with rolling countryside and an economy based on timber. Reminiscing today, Mose Sacchi, an eighty-four-year-old retired logger, recalls when the woods were full of men from the Canadian maritime provinces, logging with spool donkeys on skid roads until the mud got too deep in the winter. Across a continent, the Canadian timber men had begun again, settling not in a redundant New Nova Scotia, but making instead a deeper, tribal return to the name the Romans gave the home of the Scots.

So remote that, until 1912, the most practical means of contact with the world outside was by sea, the company developed its mill operation into a self-sustaining economic cell, treating its own water, generating its own electricity, manufacturing replacement parts and even building many of its own machines. As the mills and the town grew, so did a strong local tradition of husbandry, of the thrifty application of available skills and materials, of wasting little and wanting less.

39

Looking down through the slots and gratings in the mill floor, you can see huge heaps of sawdust and wood scraps, waste from the line collected in bins, and used as fuel for the boilers that generate the electric power not only for the mills, but for the entire town. So much lumber, sawdust, chips and scrap is scavenged by the various milling operations that, in fact, the only part of the tree now burned as waste at Scotia is the bark, which the company, working to adapt its boiler-burners, intends to use for fuel. When this happens, it will mean the end of the traditional teepee-burners at Scotia, only one of which is still in operation.

As you approach the far end of the mill, the scale of the process, if not the noise, is reduced. The machinery grows smaller, and the beamed wooden building begins to take on some of the high-ceiling emptiness of a lumber shed. What once comprised logs of varying sizes, grains and colors are now uniform pieces of lumber moving evenly along a line in flat rattles and clacks. Probably only in whaling is the raw material of an industry so much more impressive than the end product.

In a drafty corner of the building, beside the trimming machine, a row of seventeen constantly whirling circular saws, a man wearing an insulated windbreaker stands pushing levers, dropping individual blades down to cut the passing lengths of lumber in sections, trimming off the defective wood and unmarketable lengths. The level of noise is still so high that he has to leave the line to talk. This time, you sprint across a row of moving chains and, dodging lumber, go through a door in the end of the building and step onto an open platform and into sunlight so bright it makes you squint.

With the morning fog burned away, the sky is an endless, cloudless blue; the trees stand in unbroken green crowds on every hill. The noise of the mill still in your ears, you talk in an unnecessarily raised voice; between the forest and the mill it is difficult to get your bearings.

The trimmerman's name is Clare Somerville, a retired Navy man who has more than ten years with Pacific Lumber toward his second pension. He, too, has had dreams about his job, of saws falling out of control, the first couple of months he was on the line, but he's grown used to the repetitiousness of the work and the noise;

it's like a duty station aboard a ship, something that you do regularly until it becomes part of you.

Standing outside in the cool air and warm sunshine, ringed by redwoods, feeling in every nerve end the vibrations of the mill, you begin to understand what it must be like, every working day, to go from the edges of a wilderness into the noise, violence and monotony of a redwood mill. And suddenly, the order, strictness and neatness of the mill, and the polite niceness, the genuine friendliness and the desire not to offend on the part of the people that you meet begin to take on deeper meaning.

For most people who work in large-scale "heavy" industry, the surroundings that they live in provide some sort of conditioning for the work they do on the job. Reporting to a plant from a city neighborhood, a suburb where there is light industry, a union hall, or even a semi-rural area with large-scale agriculture, provides a transition from life to work, a series of gradations in which a man's life fits, just as his work fits into the compressed world of the production line. But in Humboldt County, near the Pacific Lumber Company's mills at Scotia, these cushioning stages between life and work do not exist. There is the forest, silent, still, timeless, primitive; and there is the mill, noisy, violent, regimented, complex. Each precludes the other. When you are in the mill, it seems impossible that there could be deep woods less than a mile away. When you are in the woods, this sensation is reversed. The switch in physical surroundings is so complete that it requires changing modes of physical movement, speech, hearing and even thought: a man working beside a deafeningly loud planing machine one day may well be quietly stalking a deer in the woods the next. Between these extremes, there are no conditioning stages, no city, light industry, or large farms, and, in the case of Scotia, not even a labor union. There is only the company, and the company town.

Out of this clash of opposites has been born, at Scotia, a hybrid society, a realized fantasy, a community of almost-fanatical moderation that attempts to resolve the nearly schizophrenic human alternation between working in a factory and living in a forest.

Imagine a young man, just out of high school or returned from the service, who takes a dull, repetitious job in one of the mills. On weekends, with his choice of state or national parks nearby, he goes hunting, fishing, camping or hiking. In the quiet of the forest, he is as far away from his job on the line as it is possible to get; yet, come seven-thirty Monday morning, he must go into the mill and perform like a robot. Nothing outside prepares him for that. Probably he is having nightmares about the work he is learning to do during the day. Looking forward, he might well project for himself a bleak future indeed, fluctuating between mill and woods, half-rustic and half-automaton.

But, instead, there is another future, complete in every detail, incorporating both life and work, manufactured by the company and packaged in the town, encouraging him to moderate both his needs and his desires.

After he has put in ninety days on his mill job, he can get on the list to move into Scotia, where a comfortable one-bedroom company bungalow, with a garden and a lawn on a quiet residential street rents from under sixty dollars a month. Water and sewage and garbage removal are free. Every five to seven years, the company will repaint his house, inside and out, free. As he moves up in the company, or as his family grows, he can move to a larger house in another part of town. The first year, he gets a three per cent salary bonus, gradually increasing to seven per cent. He has good accident and health coverage, and a choice of a pension plan or an investment program. More than almost any other company, Pacific Lumber promotes nearly entirely from within, and although he is starting a long way from the expensive machines of the mill and the redwood panelling of the main office, he knows that there are men in those places who began where he did. And, in the remote future, as a Pacific Lumber employee, if his son or daughter qualifies for a four-year college, he or she will receive a thousand-dollar scholarship from the company.

Against this deeper backdrop, the daily scene played out in the mills becomes part of a more significant drama, and the near-automaton doing millwork begins to feel himself a whole man. A dull, repetitive job that earns you a better house in a more pleasant neighborhood than you could afford elsewhere doesn't seem so dumb after all. A day spent silently tending a noisy machine can't be considered wasted when it is helping to pay for a college education for your children. Even the woods, with their silence and freedom, seem more available to you because of your work in the nearby mill.

Presented a life of moderated extremes, a picture of balance and wholeness, a man goes on the line and waits, measuring out the days in lengths of raw, green lumber, waiting his chance to become a sawyer, a trimmerman, an edgerman, or escape into the main office, patience gradually flexing firm, ambition slightly softening.

If, however, he chooses to reject the moderate's course, if he is frequently absent from work, guilty of drunkenness, fighting or reckless driving, if he is an offensive neighbor, mistreats his family, or gets himself heavily into debt, he will feel the pull of the company reins. A man who has applied for a house in Scotia may be kept waiting six months, a year, or forever, because of his behavior; a man living in a company house, who fails to give the yard a minimum of care, may find a company garden crew coming by to cut his lawn and weed his flowers for him, a service for which he will be billed. The pressure is subtle, but firm.

In the *Phaedrus*, Plato compares the soul to a pair of winged horses driven by a charioteer. One horse is upright and cleanly made, with lofty neck and aquiline nose, the other a crooked, lumbering animal, shag-eared and deaf; one responds to guidance by word and admonition, the other, heedless of the whip, plunges and runs away. Together, they give the charioteer all manner of trouble until, by urging both horses forward and reining them in, the one willing and unresisting, the other unruly and wanton, the intractable horse tires, is tamed and humbled, and thereafter follows the will of the charioteer.

Let the upright horse stand for the redwood forest, the brutish animal the mills, the charioteer and his reins the company and the town, and you begin to understand how, by moderating the harsh character of the mills with the order and restraint of the town, the company has established a balance between the pounding machine world of the mills and the dawn primitiveness of the redwood forest.

"I was a big goof-off in school," says Corky Kemp, timekeeper in the machine shop at Scotia. "And I went to work feeding the sander in the plywood plant, just pushing buttons, switching a machine on and off. It was hard to stay alert. I wasn't happy, but I liked the company. You have to work somewhere, and this is a pretty good place. I got hurt twice in three weeks, and the second time it cost 'em a good deal of money, but they never bug you about it or try to get rid of you.

"I went and talked to Personnel and told them what I wanted to do. Mr. Hunsaker told me he'd call me when he had an opening, and, by God, he did."

Corky lives with his pretty wife and two young children in a company house in town, for which Pacific Lumber deducts eighty-five dollars a month from his check for rent, water and garbage. He pays no personal property tax. When something goes wrong with his household plumbing, if one of

48

the kids breaks a window or the electricity goes out, Corky just calls the company plumbing shop or the carpentry shop or the electrical shop, a man is sent out promptly, and there is no bill. Recently, the company helped him remodel his patio, delivering the building materials Corky had bought, then sending a crew over to lay gravel and pour cement.

"Some guys don't want to move into Scotia. They say it's too much like living at work. There isn't much to do here, and some people like to go more, do more things. Golly, for the rent, you can't match this. Living here, you actually have the opportunity and the money to do a little more. They keep the place the way you want it, all they ask is that you take fairly good care of it. The only way I'd move out of town is if I'd buy a place. But what I hear about taxes and stuff, I think I'd rather stay."

Corky is twenty-four years old. "I got forty-one years to go, and I can't see any reason I'd leave."

49

At exactly twelve o'clock, the whistles in Mill A, Mill B, the remill, the planing mill and the plywood mill all hoot at once, and the peculiar sound of the mills—a combination of deadweight rumbling, metallic screeches and unexplainable electric whines and groans that together somehow suggest the childhood city sound of old, heavy streetcars—fades into the quiet of the woods.

Inside the sprawling wooden buildings, in the factory, on the log pond, in the offices and in the lumber storage yard and even among the crews out in the trees, everything is abruptly silent and still, as in a film where the sound has failed and the motion is frozen. In one great orchestration of hundreds of digestive tracts, a whole community eats lunch. Along the streets leading to the mills, drivers curb their trucks and, unwrapping sandwiches, accelerate their appetites. In the shade beneath the eaves of the mills and sheds, men sit with their lunches in rows on railroad ties, steps, the ground, while the residential streets, suddenly busy with walking, driving or bicycling men, grow quiet and empty again as the last man disappears into his house.

Outside the machine shop, in a series of thin clanks, a pair of men start tossing horseshoes in a pit beside the corrugated steel wall, while down by the river, a man in hastily slipped-on waders makes a quick noontime cast of his flyrod, hoping to catch one of the salmon that are rumored to be running upstream.

On the partition that separates his desk from the clanging and scraping of the machine shop, Corky Kemp keeps a plaque, proclaiming his own sentiments in a way that seems to sum up the spirit of insistent moderation that motivates the company, the reining-in of life that preserves the balance between the contained violence of the mills and the close stillness of the forest, and has formed the character of the company town. The plaque reads: "It's nice to be important, but it's more important to be nice."

the town

In the town of Scotia there are streets and buildings existing so completely outside time that they have become vessels of the unconscious, provoking a sense of *déjà vu* that is almost paralyzing in its intensity. There is the street you grew up on, the house, the lawn—not the way it is now, or even the way it was then—but the way it could have been if only the world had held still, just a little. Nothing seems to have aged or changed. Nothing looks very old or very new. Removed from the extremes of millwork and woods, the moderated life seems here to have reached its fullest expression in these modest, pastel-painted, amenable wooden frame bungalows, built between 1910 and 1925, with their open front porches, unfenced front yards, gardens, and rich patina of care, almost like the surviving Victorians of San Francisco. There is a comforting feel of proportion to the houses, a sense of having been planned to human and not automotive scale. There are no driveways or discarded wrecks out in front, and small children play freely in the street. At times, you can almost hear the voices of your own childhood, network radio programs, the admonitions of friends and family dead; the air is thick with unsatisfied desire.

In a vacant house on Williams Street, just below the log pond, two men in painters' whites are repainting interior enamel in colors selected by the house's new occupants. In the background, music from a portable radio echoes through the empty rooms and over the dropcloths, accompanied by the smell of fresh coffee from the kitchen. There is a relaxed feel of working by the job instead of by the clock, of patient attention to a craft. Unlike the men in the mills, the painters aren't dwarfed and muted by their work.

The men, Bill Byker and Harry Crofoot, work as a team, going from house to house, painting walls and woodwork that have been done over so many times that sometimes the paint is slow to set. Working in these quiet, pleasant surroundings for more than fifteen years, both men have formed an attachment to the company and the town that is deep, emotional and genuine, and an easy conversational relationship that fits the self-imposed rhythms of their work. When one of the men wants to talk, he just sets aside his brush.

"I grew up in a small town in Minnesota," says Harry Crofoot, "and back there if you wanted something, you could ask your neighbor for it or even go and get it if nobody was home. In the city, they'd have the law on you. If you like life in a small town and don't mind your neighbor looking at you, it's a wonderful place to live."

Bill Byker, the other painter, is a tall, gentle, vulnerable man with an unmotivated generosity and sweetness that would make him automatically suspect if you met him in a large city. Perhaps the flower children of a few years back possessed something of this quality, before the hard drugs, panhandling and hepatitis, but with Byker it's personal and individual, with no ideological freight attached. Do you need a place to stay? There is room at his house. A place to take a shower? Shoot some pool? He offers to let you use his card at the Scotia Men's Club. The town, to Byker, is his home, and a stranger is, first of all, a guest.

Seen from a vacant company house, life in Scotia seems to approach an egalitarian ideal. There is no furniture—or lack of furniture—to declare individual tastes, no clothes or pictures, no expensive appliances or second-hand castoffs. The walls and woodwork of one house differ only in pastel tone from the walls and woodwork of the occupied house next door; the douglas-fir floors, sanded and varnished countless times over the years, all have the same red-blond tone. Through the window, the unfenced lawns merge seamlessly with one another. To an outsider's eye, there seems to be little distinction between one single-story, shingle-roof, wooden house in Scotia and another, or even from block to block.

But as you talk to the people who live in the houses, stop them on the street to ask directions, sit with them in their homes, or simply observe the way they speak about certain sections of the town, it becomes clear that if the obvious extremes of wealth and poverty—mansions, slums—do not exist in Scotia, it isn't because the utopian dream of the judge and the garbage collector living side by side has been realized.

Within the overall conformations of the town, all sorts of subtle social distinctions exist; everyone is aware of them, and to some people they are extremely important.

59

One street is considered the most desirable to live on, largely because people have traditionally maintained their houses better there. Another street has been looked down upon since the days when Italian and Portuguese families used its backyards to raise vegetables. Certain houses, built for company executives, are considered highly desirable, although their advantages may consist of nothing more than a fireplace, a closed-in sunporch and an extra bedroom. There seems to be some correlation between a man's position with the company and the size and location of the house he is assigned. In addition to this subtle local pecking order, there is, beyond the town, what amounts to a landed, titled aristocracy.

Years ago, in acquiring huge tracts of land when land was cheap, the company came into ownership of several large ranches outside the immediate vicinity of the town, and some of this property has become a sort of country seat for the directors, secluded lodges used for summer residences or for entertaining visitors of a certain stature, and open to employees at the middle-management level by invitation as a sign of appreciation and interest. These invitations, conferred discreetly, are prized by the people who receive them above any other privileges the company bestows. And, even among employees who have never visited them, the lodges are spoken of with an almost monarchial awe, the way a medieval serf might regard the castle of his sovereign.

As long as these social distinctions remain, the company can work the reins of the town to maximum effect, rewarding individual performance and ambition with a more desirable house or a hunting weekend, while preserving the visible sense of common identity that unites the company, the workers and the town. In effect, the company is offering its employees life both ways: there is enough personal recognition available for the competitively inclined, with fringe-benefits enough to satisfy the most insecure. Little wonder that, with a staff at Scotia of nearly a thousand people, Pacific Lumber's turnover averages less than six per cent a year.

In a house just up the street from where the painters are working, two teenage girls are staying together while the parents of one of the girls are away. Like many people who spend a good deal of time together, the girls have begun to resemble one another, with similar hair styles and dress and certain shared mannerisms. Both girls are pretty, somewhat shy, polite, and prone to giggling. Both plan to leave Scotia and go live and work someplace else.

For teenagers, and for teenage girls in particular, there is simply nothing to do in Scotia. The Winema Theatre (built entirely of redwood and, in its carved beams, detailed coves of walls, moulding and scrollwork, probably the only movie house in the world that looks better with the lights on), once owned and operated by the company, presented its last double feature in the late fifties, when a combination of TV, sagging attendance and charges of youth vandalism drove it into a darkness broken now only by a rare volunteer firemen's dance, bingo game, or church-sponsored film. The Scotia skating rink, which overlooked the Eel River, was not overlooked *by* the river, which swept the rink away in the disastrous flood of 1955.

The skating rink was not replaced, and the Scotia baseball park, which was, was destroyed by the even worse flood of 1964. This second flood, the most catastrophic in California's history, all but ended the spontaneous social life of the community, left the young people of the town without a place to informally gather, and made the minimum evening social requirement a twenty-seven-mile drive to the nearest city, Eureka.

The things that are most visible about young people elsewhere—beards, long hair, racial and sexual emancipation, psychedelic clothing, peace symbols, clenched fists—are all but invisible here. Women are losing, not gaining, employment opportunities in the plywood mill, where the handful of women held over from a plant acquired by Pacific Lumber from another company are replaced by men as they leave. The town's—and the company's—racial minorities seem limited to a single Indian in the main office and a few Mexicans in the locomotive shop, though as far back as 1903 the mill crew included both Negroes and Filipinos, against whom the whites went on strike in protest. And a rock festival, held in Eureka, proved the ultimate fizzle by attracting mostly adults.

For girls, in the summer or on weekends, there is only the most meager choice of things to do: cook, sew, read, work in the laundry. At least the boys can hunt, fish, or go down by the river and drink beer. A swimming area, bulldozed out of the river down below the railroad tracks, was not restored after the 1964 flood, and the pool in the community center is booked almost entirely for organized groups and swimming lessons.

Indeed, the woman in town who seems to have made the fullest adjustment to life in Scotia is a lady named Tonia, now in her seventies, who smokes cigars, swears, fishes, drives a pickup, doesn't own a dress and, in addition to raising her own family, worked on the company railroad, bossing a section gang.

"When we were kids, we made our own fun," says a woman who was a girl in Scotia forty years ago, in criticism of today's young.

True. But according to Fred Elliott, a third-generation Scotian and the town's most knowledgeable historian, there was more fun to be made.

"There was no freeway, so there were orchards up on the hill and creeks to play in. I used to play up on the hill all the time. Nobody had much money, and we very seldom went downtown. A movie was twelve cents, and it cost twenty cents to go skating. People used to have their own milk cows, and practically everybody had his own vegetable garden in an area the company would plow up every spring. The kids used to put wood in the houses for heat and cooking, and they'd mow lawns—that was the best way to earn money. Now everybody has power lawn-mowers."

As Fred Elliott speaks of Scotia's past, he is literally surrounded by it. In a rear room of his company house on Main Street, Fred keeps a collection of local cultural and historical relics: armchairs, ornate tables, an armoire, bellflower phonographs, albums of old photos, portraits, letters, bills of sale, notes, deeds, and other curiosities. Sitting in an antique armchair, his hair parted down the middle, wearing steel-rimmed glasses, holding his dog on his lap, Fred looks like the proprietor of a small and rather funky antique store.

"Whenever anybody who's lived a long time in town moves out and throws stuff away, I always go and look through it," Fred says, pointing out valuables in the room he has acquired as castoffs.

Listening to Fred talk about the history of the town, sensing his fondness for his collection ("I couldn't become an antique dealer," he admits. "I can't stand getting rid of any of my stuff."), it is easy to imagine him teaching school, clerking in the main office, or, more appropriately, as curator of the Scotia Museum. Then he tells you that he spends his day driving a lumber carrier in the company yards. And suddenly the two sides of the man—one poring quietly over old, florid handwriting and fading county directories, the other bouncing along fifteen feet in the air on a carrier straddling stacks of lumber—no longer seem to fit together. His job and his life seem to fly apart, merging again only as he goes more deeply into the subject of his collecting.

On a secluded country road not far from Scotia, Fred has built what amounts to a private museum, constructing from scratch a Victorian cottage, all white gingerbread and lacy trim, resembling a movie set in its pristine oldness, completely furnished with a brass bed, antique furniture and historical curiosities, and topped by two flagpoles, one flying the American flag and one, in honor of the local Norwegian Club, of which Fred is president, Norway's.

Fred has never spent a night in his house, and his wife refuses to live there. It has no electricity. But early on a Saturday morning, or on a weekday evening in summer or early fall when it is still light, Fred drives out along the wooded road to his place in the country, puts on his big straw hat and his rubber boots, and spends three, maybe four hours puttering, attending to the house, the garden, the furniture, or the old cars, wagons and fire equipment, in varying stages of restoration, that he keeps in a shed nearby.

Fred Elliott's elaborate puttering is more than just a pastime, a counterweight to the monotony of his job; it's a declaration of selfhood in the face of the homogenized character of the company and the town, a personal indulgence where self-denial is the rule, an expression of not caring what people think in an atmosphere of "niceness" and politeness, as well as the foundations for a life of his own to go to when his days as a PL employee have come to an end.

More than most younger people in Scotia, Fred is aware of the rapid personal disintegration that often follows retirement from the company, of the men who've worked in good health all their lives, looking forward to the day when their time would be their own, to the retirement that comes to represent the reward for "staying on" twenty, thirty, or forty years, only to die or grow senile within a year or two after leaving their jobs.

Here, when a man retires, he faces the loss not only of his work, but of his house, his community, and the whole controlling influence of his life.

70

Traditionally when people grew old and retired from the company, they were required to move out of Scotia. This was not callously done; there were no evictions and little pressure was applied, but there was an understanding that once a family contained no active Pacific Lumber employee, that family had a period of about a year to find housing someplace else. Only about a third of Pacific Lumber's employees actually live in Scotia, and there was, and is, a list of people waiting to move into the town. But now there are perhaps a dozen retired Pacific Lumber employees living in company houses—more than there have ever been at one time before. Some of the people have been in retirement for as long as seven years, and have no immediate plans of moving. The housing policy has been relaxed, apparently because among the retirees is the mother of one of the company's chief executives. For the older people who remain, the living conditions—low rent, cheap utilities, minimum upkeep—are unbeatable. But no one really knows what will happen when the executive's mother is gone. And the fact remains that Scotia, a community complete in almost every other respect, conspicuously lacks a graveyard.

The retired man who lingers on in the town tends to dangle either motionless or fruitlessly hyperactive between life and death. On the weekdays of retirement, the mill whistle still blows as it did on the weekdays of work. During mill hours, the streets are empty of other men. The community, with its reverse-gear civic planning, where it is the mills that sprawl and the residential areas that are limited and concentrated, seems to no longer have any place for him. There seems to be no gathering spot devoted just to leisure. He doesn't even like to be seen just sitting outside his house. Every street he walks down leads to work he cannot do; the sidewalks are empty of everyone except small children. Hearing the noises of the mill while he himself sits idle, realizing there are people on the waiting list who would like to move into his house, a man feels half-sick or disabled already.

Sitting amid samples from his collection, talking about the old-timers who so often die or "go dippy" when they retire, Fred Elliott begins to take on the character of a classic Downeaster, part stubborn individualist and part pixie. It seems as though, after three generations in Scotia, the Elliott family has developed a resistant strain to the endemic local tradition of moderation, inconspicuousness and concealed individuality and that, as represented by Fred, the Elliotts are determined to survive as distinct persons, while taking a whimsical and almost subversive pleasure in doing so.

"I wouldn't take an indoor job," says Fred Elliott, speaking of his work in the company yard. "Even for more money. I'd rather be outside on my own."

Suddenly, it seems possible that Fred Elliott, driving about the Scotia yards on his lumber carrier, with his solitude, physical mobility, freedom from regimentation, time to daydream about his house, his antiques, his albums and his old vehicles, and even, fifteen feet above the ground, his view, actually enjoys his job.

For other people in Scotia, finding your own answer to life in a world that seems to begin and end with the company and the town is not quite so easy; to have personal goals beyond what is available within the local life-situation is to be critical of it; little wonder that an ambitious or individualistic boy or girl is apt to be considered somewhat freakish. For girls especially, the emotional cost of living in what is still overwhelmingly a man's world seems terribly high. Not surprisingly, many local girls, financially or intellectually unable to keep up with school, or simply growing desperate with boredom, get married when they are seniors in high school or go to work in a store. They have discovered that this is the way things are, and that's that. Digging in, married and with children and still in their early twenties in a community where, every year, it gets a little harder to leave and a little easier to stay, they feel the pressure—social, financial, psychological—until it gradually gets to them, and they scale down their aspirations to the limits of the town.

73

Up at the other end of Main Street from where Fred Elliott lives, inside the Scotia Museum, pretty Kathy Fletcher asks a man in a vacation-wear windbreaker to write his name and hometown in the visitors book, then hands the man a wallet-size slug of redwood printed with instructions on how to get to Mill B.

The museum, a redwood Hellenic building with columns of redwood log complete with bark outside, and glass cases filled mostly with old photographs of railroad rolling stock inside, was once the Scotia First National Bank, and high above the polished floor there are still peepholes through which the bank manager, sitting every payday with a rifle in his lap, used to watch for robbers as the paymaster tendered employees their wages in cash below. Today, the building is used mainly to divert Scotia's considerable tourist traffic—forty thousand visitors a year—away from the company's main office.

Amazingly, by asking visitors to register at the museum, giving them permits and instructions on how to reach Mill B, and by mounting explanatory signs along the catwalks through the mill, Pacific Lumber is able to run its entire tourist operation with a staff of one person.

74

That person, Kathy, an unusually ambitious girl of about twenty with china-doll good looks, hair in bangs above dark, luminous eyes, is a student at Brigham Young University in Utah, where she is preparing to enter library work—but not in Humboldt County. The daughter of a man who works in one of the mills, Kathy, who quite obviously could have found someone to settle down with locally, has broken out of the circle of mill town/high school/marriage/mill town, but only through her own extraordinary energy and will.

Each weekday and Saturday in summer, after putting in a full day greeting and directing tourists at the museum, taking time only to change clothes, Kathy drives down below the mill pond to Bertain's Laundry, where, skipping dinner, she puts in another full shift, taking clothes out of a steam press until ten or eleven at night. Coolly, she has studied her career prospects in patriarchal Humboldt County, estimated the price of her passage, and determined to pay it. By working up to eighty-one hours a week, while the girls who were her high-school classmates mind children, choose furniture, and send husbands off to work in the mills, she is financing the professional credential that will be her ticket out.

"The kids here are secure within an insecurity," says a teacher in the Scotia Elementary School. "They don't believe anything could ever change. Hell, it's been that way to most families for two or three generations. What they don't know is that PL could fold tomorrow. And then what?"

Most people, accepting the situation in Scotia as it is, recognizing that Pacific Lumber with its high-quality line of products and enormous timber holdings is not about to fail overnight, decide to cope with things as they are, and settle for the obvious rewards of a relatively comfortable and untroubled future.

"Why go someplace else, when PL is so good to me here?" is a sentiment you hear expressed again and again. Only rarely do you pick up an admission of frustration or regret.

"My pop doesn't say much about it, but he's sorry he dropped out of college and came up here," says the son of a man in middle-management, working temporarily in the mills while he is between schools.

"He's doing all right, has a good deal, makes good money, doesn't bust his ass. But he's still sorry. You can tell. If I quit school and came back here to work, he'd throw my ass out of the house."

83

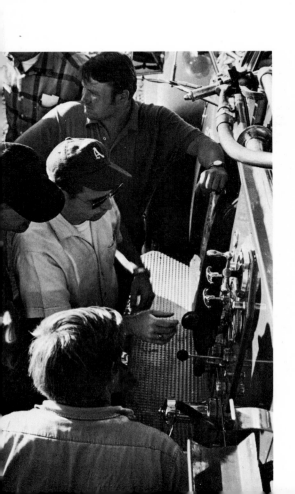

At the Scotia Volunteer Fire Station, a well-kept one-story pale green building on Main Street, about half the men of the department, wearing green uniform shirts, have gathered to have their pictures taken. Charlie Langdon, the fire chief, has blown the company whistle to call them here, and there is a lot of ribbing about false alarms amid the self-conscious tucking-in and buttoning-up of the rarely worn officials shirts. The department's two pumpers and one hook-and-ladder have been pulled out in front of the building, and the men are standing on the equipment in groups suggested by the photographer. In a distant way, they resemble another photograph on a wall of the Scotia museum, a picture of the old volunteers, with almost contemporary muttonchop whiskers and handlebar moustaches, posing stiffly with hand-drawn equipment and dalmatian.

In a town made almost entirely of wood, with miles of forest all around and yards full of stacked, drying lumber, the thought of fire is never far from anybody's mind. Scotia had a disastrous fire in 1895, and a community which gets by without a single local policeman today supports a firefighting crew of sixty volunteers.

85

With the closing of the theater, the passing of the Scotia Lumberjacks baseball team, the Scotia park and the skating rink, the fire department has become the center of what remains of the town's social life, planning and organizing the two or three dances that the community has each year, doing charity work, helping get out the vote during elections; it's about the only place where men can meet man-to-man outside the routine of work.

Traditionally, there has been a waiting list to get on the fire department, but according to one authority, the pool for firemen is limited now by the large percentage of Seventh-day Adventists, Mormons, and members of the Assembly of God in town, who don't drink, dance, or socialize on Saturday, when all the department's functions take place.

Gradually, the men standing on the trucks get into place, fall quiet, stare individually at the camera, and the pictures are taken. The men are frozen in their collective moment like the men on the museum wall in their muttonchop whiskers. Afterward, they linger awhile, talking easily among themselves, seeming not at all reluctant to be giving up a Saturday morning until, when it is clear that there is nothing more to hold them, the Scotia Volunteer Fire Department diffuses into thirty private lives.

89

The elegant old man has been walking the streets of the town every day, smiling and alert, playing with children, followed by dogs. He has brown, lively eyes, skin the color of lightly stained lumber, a cotton-white moustache and neatly combed white hair, and he smokes a movie-gambler's small cigar. He smiles frequently and nods when spoken to, and he speaks in an unnecessarily loud voice.

"You know that machine in the factory, the planing machine? The one with the house around it? Fifty years I worked on that machine. Fifty years."

As if for emphasis, he smiles and nods again, his eyes illuminating his face. The planing machinery of a lumber mill operates at a level of shrieking noise that has been discovered to be beyond the decibel count tolerable to the human ear. Now, under the provisions of California's Walsh-Healy Act, the planing machines are gradually being enclosed in small soundproof rooms on the mill floor, with the men who operate them standing outside, feeding and catching the lumber through slots.

A moment later, after nodding his agreement to stay, the old man abruptly gets up and walks off, heading home. He is deaf as a post, a walking industrial accident.

Just inside the entrance of the Scotia Men's Club, Dwight Eisenhower stares down out of a frame. Not Eisenhower the statesman, the familiar father figure of the fifties, but a returned-hero Eisenhower, in full military uniform, draped with sashes and glittering medals, arm fixed in a stern salute. A conqueror.

Suddenly, it is 1946, and America is victorious, powerful, righteous, and just. Its people still practice a wartime self-denial, anticipating satisfactions long deferred, pausing before a binge. The rooms are dark and spare, windows venetian blinded, walls papered only above the thumbprint-and-hair-oil high-water line. On a board the members' names are carefully mounted in individual tabs; nearby is an open guestbook whose most recent signature is two years old.

In the reading room, a lone man, on his lunch break from one of the mills, sits among empty wooden armchairs, reading the morning *Chronicle*, his hat on a hook outside the door. The pool tables are empty, and one of the green cloths is torn. From a backroom comes the raffish banter of a card game.

Back in the days when Scotia was still a raw mill town, and there were crews of loggers living in the woods who came into town and got paid in gold coin, the community supported a semi-official hook shop—a combination whorehouse, saloon and gambling joint known as the Green Goose—which the company tolerated as a sort of a carnal safety valve. But with the coming of Local Option near the end of World War I, and the closing of the Green Goose, came a heated and company-kindled moral reaction that turned the town dry and kept it dry even after Repeal. Only in recent years was a cocktail lounge permitted in the basement of the Scotia Inn, in a converted ice cream parlor, and the trade there is mostly hotel guests and salesmen.

In the place of the Green Goose, the company hatched a bird of another feather, a YMCA-style alternative, the Men's Club: an idealized attempt to keep unmarried lumbermen both interested and satisfied in a complete absence of sin. Though all seven hundred and fifty of the company's male employees are eligible to join, the club rooms echo with emptiness. Perhaps when the community was isolated, pool, cards, table tennis,

hot showers, magazines and newspapers were diversion enough, but that was in the days before automatic machinery in the mills and chain saws and tractors in the forest left men the time and energy to seek entertainment outside of town. Nowadays, the men of Scotia, like the kids, feel an itch the town can't scratch.

In the backroom, four men are performing today's installment of a fast, noisy, serialized pinochle game, while a fifth man watches, eating his lunch. One of the players is loud, constantly chattering, working hard to swagger while seated in a chair. Ignoring his barbs, the man across the table stares silently at his cards. Between them are two young men who look and dress like college students of just a few years back, and who bear a strong facial resemblance. Brothers, they have both grown up in the area, attended local colleges, and have come to work for the company, as did their father, his brother, and their father before them.

Generation frequently succeeds generation on the Pacific Lumber payroll, partly through necessity ("There's PL, PG&E [the gas and electric company] and the phone company," explains one of the brothers), but also due, in part, to an enduring sense of paternal affiliation. Remoteness, self-sufficiency, and the paternalistic attitude of Pacific Lumber toward its employees have given local life the patriarchal flavor of a chiefdom.

93

95

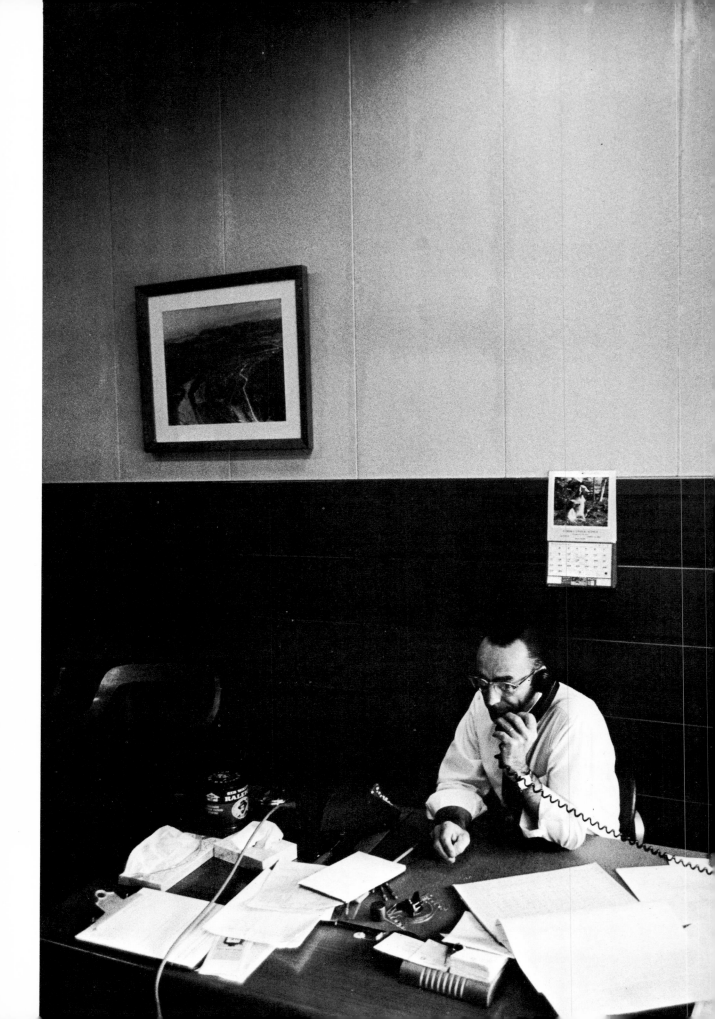

"People have more chance to grow up with their kids here," says Bill Crofoot. And it's true, at least for men. Of the physical advantages life in Humboldt County offers—hunting, fishing, camping—all are traditional activities of fathers and sons. In summer, employees' sons are given first crack at fifty to a hundred temporary jobs that the company has to fill, and most of the young men in the town gradually acquire the attitude that when they leave school or the service or give up trying to construct a new life in a strange town, there will always be a job for them at PL.

"I just never considered anything else," a third-generation employee admits.

Working for the same company, people tend to settle in the same town, living sometimes on the same streets and even in the same houses as their parents did. Visiting relatives is still a big weekend social activity. And if things sometimes seem a little cliqueish or inbred, there is always the reassuring example of those who left the chiefdom and have come to regret it.

"My daughter couldn't wait to get out of Scotia," says a local woman, standing in her kitchen amid jars of preserved pickles and a cooling apple pie. "Now she lives in San José, her children are just starting school, and she'd give anything to be back."

The totem of this tribal feeling, the symbol of the blood relationship of family, land and company, is the town itself.

"I lived outside town for five years," says cost supervisor Martin Marks, sitting in the living room of his comfortable home overlooking Mill B. "We bought a house in Fortuna, but it just wasn't the same. You just didn't have the sense of commonness that you have here. My kids say that here it feels like home."

Below, his community spreads out before him, a tangible present, a visible past, There is the light-green administration building where Martin's office is; stretching off to the left is the mill where he makes his daily rounds, gathering data for cost

99

analyses and incentive rewards. To the rear of the mill is the Green Chain, where Martin worked in 1947, and just beyond, the yards where in 1964 the river came in and went out with a loss of seasoned lumber in board feet that Martin tallied in the millions. Off to the right is the Scotia shopping center, where a handy concentration of local enterprises, food store, pharmacy, variety store, gas station, lunch counter—once operated by the company—are now leased to outside managers. And on the street directly below his house is the school his children attended, with the foundations of the new Scotia elementary school beside it.

There is a soothing oneness to it all, a continuity among the essentials of life that seems infinitely reassuring, evidence of having made the right choices. Perhaps because of it, Marks and his wife (she is still in the same house she lived in before they were married) radiate an openness and generosity that is almost impossible to compare to anything on the outside.

"I grew up in Southern California," says Martin Marks, "and after World War Two, I could see the modern rat-race coming, and I wanted to get out. I went on a vacation drive up through the valley and came north through Scotia. When I returned to Southern California, I made up my mind to come back here and live."

Marks had been an assistant personnel manager of a boat-building firm in Los Angeles. He arrived in Humboldt County in the middle of the redwood industry's worst strike, when most of the mills were shut down completely.

"I talked to a lot of people. The friendliness was something you just couldn't measure. There were guys out in the woods trying to get by making split products, but nobody was hauling them. So I bought a truck and went into the trucking business. We bought in the woods and sold in the valley to grape growers. It was rugged work, but good, clean, wholesome. After a time I went to work for the company, on the Green Chain."

Now, hunting and fishing every season, spending weekends in a family cabin on Lake Ruth, with a good job about a five-minute walk from his house, happily married to an extraordinary woman he wouldn't have met if he hadn't moved here, living in a town that he knows will look pretty much the same in fifteen or twenty years, removed from a world that seems increasingly deranged, Martin Marks savors the taste of his own past decisions and leaves the future in the hands of the company.

The school that Martin Marks looks down on warmly ("It was like school when I was a boy. You knew all the teachers and all the kids.") is a folksy, gray shingle building that has been condemned for four years and will soon be replaced by a modern structure in the shape of a triple hexagon.

In a town where very little changes, the new school represents the biggest innovation in years, not just architecturally, but because it will depart from the town's traditionally conservative educational pattern to use new techniques such as interclass groupings and a library learning center.

"We're going to have to do an educational job on the parents as well as on the children," says a member of the Scotia school board, anticipating resistance.

Another man connected with the school is less optimistic. He feels the new building, with its lack of disciplinary corners to stand children in, won't make it, because "The old teachers are too stubborn."

In Mrs. Campbell's fifth grade classroom, the children are getting a sample of the new technique, breaking up into several discussion groups, each of which must prepare a position on a contemporary social issue: welfare, conservation, women's lib. The class is small, only about twenty-five children, but there is enthusiastic noise, the sound of heated discussion, of children sorting out, probably for the first time, their own opinions from those of their parents and friends.

The teacher, Cynthia Campbell, grew up in Scotia, where her mother grew up and her father is a vice president of the company. A tall, striking ex-model who wears mod clothes well, she is married to a man from Australia whom she met in San Francisco. Now, they have both decided to settle in Scotia, where her husband has started in the mill operation.

When the spokesmen from the children's discussion groups rise to make their reports in question-and-answer fashion, the replies are lively, interested, and carry a strongly local flavor.

"Women can't work on the Green Chain," begins the women's lib group spokeswoman.

Watching the children respond to genuine issues and react to stimuli from the world outside, you realize that, if the new school is really used properly, it will change things. Scotia isn't an oppressive place for a child to grow up, but it is strict; the company has rules about trespassing, motorcycles, Everything. Everybody seems to know what his neighbor's kids are up to. In time, some of these ideas and assumptions will be challenged. Young minds will be blown. Yet most of these children will stay in the area. Few of their families will have the wherewithal to

102

send them on to college. Probably they will be housewives and blue-collar workers. But perhaps housewives and workers of a different sort than inhabit Scotia now.

"The children are naive, but smart," says vivacious Peggy Rice, who teaches fourth grade. Married to a rancher in Fortuna, Peggy taught on the East Cost, and has been at the Scotia school for five years. She is aware of the limitations of local life that will keep most of her students from doing much with what they learn here. It isn't only the students who are isolated, she points out. The teacher before her taught fourth grade in Scotia for forty years and could recognize personality traits passed down two and three generations among her pupils.

According to Buzz Lincoln, Scotia's burly, gray-haired school superintendent, Pacific Lumber will own the new school building, but there is no company interference with the operation of the school or the content of the curriculum.

"The school administration and the school board are completely independent. The board is elected by the people of the town, and anyone in the district can run for the board whether he's an employee of the company or not."

Nevertheless, because of the one-industry nature of the town, there is a strong identification between the company and the school. Much of the instruction seems blue-collar in tone ("If two men load a truck in two hours. . . ."). Because the number of houses in town remains the same, the school enrollment is fairly constant, and the student body isn't seasoned with transfers coming in and out. And of the school board's current membership, all are employees of Pacific Lumber.

When Peggy Rice asks her class, "How many of you would like to live in Scotia and work for Pacific Lumber when you grow up?" nearly all the boys raise their hands. And so do half the girls.

In an increasingly abstract world, the lure of the concrete reality of Scotia remains strong. The mill whistle will sound tomorrow just as it did on any weekday morning thirty years ago; there is always a job at PL; the faithful wait to embrace the repentant; new horror stories about life on the outside are always welcome.

Not surprisingly, the list of people from Scotia who have distinguished themselves in the wider world is practically blank. Though the town's population is around a thousand, it has been at that figure for most of this century, and for many years Scotia was second only to Eureka in size; yet apart from the owners of the company itself, Scotia has yet to produce its first millionaire, scientist, inventor, philosopher, composer, painter, author, or big-league ballplayer. Where likenesses are valued, there may be little competition, but there is also little pressure to excel. Where frustrations are few, so are fantasies; a clergyman, new to the town, says he has yet to encounter an alcoholic, and no one can remember a major Scotia crime. No one sinks, but no one soars. What Scotia is really offering those dismayed with the world outside, the tie that pulls men back who vowed to leave, is not the promise of fulfillment but an assurance of moderation, the possibility of living a humane life in a humane community. And for that, there will always be a waiting list.

106

the woods

Out of the bend in the narrow, crushed-rock road falls an avalanche of Diesel cab, sixteen-tired trailer and deadweight redwood log, roaring around the turn on the wrong side to keep the shoulder from breaking down, barrel-assing into the straightaway with, if not a clear road, at least a clear conscience: anyone out here ought to have sense enough to get the hell out of the way.

The windshield of the pickup, filled one instant by a huge, square Peterbilt radiator, tilts upward the next and turns green as, all four wheels driving, we crunch up and over the bank and fallen branches and stop in a dead-end of brush as, at the same moment, with a rush of air and gargling Diesel exhaust, cab, bark-dragging log and rattling trailer all hurtle on past, leaving an underwater silence and a slowly settling pall of dust.

"Now," says Larry McCollum, sweating at the wheel, but grinning with satisfaction, "you see why we don't let people drive out here?"

We are about twenty-five miles northwest of the Pacific Lumber Company mills at Scotia, near the north fork of the Elk River, heading for one of three or four "sides"—full-scale timber operations—the company has running at any one time.

For the past half-hour, frequently dodging the loaded lumber trucks which storm along these supposedly deserted logging roads at about forty miles an hour, we have been driving through cutover land, dense with trees and brush and huge, squat red-wood stumps, land which McCollum, Pacific Lumber's forest manager, says was logged out over eighty years ago. A leathery, squint-lined straight talker with the looks and smoking habits of a Marlboro man, McCollum would rather not be out here at all. He is responsible for the daily care and feeding of all of Pacific Lumber's 167,000 timber acres, and a day spent taking people through the woods means a day's work that he'll have to make up later. But it's public relations, one of the vaguely distasteful duties—like flushing trespassing hippies out of the woods—that seem to be creeping into his job with increasing frequency. So McCollum puts himself out for strangers, answering questions and pointing things out without really knowing for sure what they think of what they're seeing.

Along the road the history of redwood logging is written in the forest to both sides. Down near the highway, just beyond the gate with the yard-high sign threatening trespassers with prosecution, down where the biggest stumps and thickest brush are, is where they did the early logging, falling trees with double-edged axes and two-man whipsaws, hauling the logs out with teams of oxen over skid roads of smaller logs, clear-cutting everything on the horizon on the assumption that the trees would never grow again, "opening up the land" to thick, jungle growth.

Farther up, we pass an old base camp, a cluster of one-story barracks-like wooden buildings—alone in the woods as a witch's cottage—a couple of bunkhouses, a cook-house, a blacksmith's shop, and a corral, where men walked in with bedrolls and lived ten or eleven months out of the year, until winter rains drove them back to town. In those days, the woods crews—choppers, riggers, chasers, bull chokers, donkey drivers, whistle punks—numbered in the hundreds, before the internal combustion engine spread from the mills out into the trees. Now part of a swearless,

sweatless Boy Scout camp, the red clapboard buildings are decorated with logging's rusting relics: two-man whip and circular saws.

Up higher, on a ridge from where forested mountains stretch west like waves in a green, endless sea, sits an old steam donkey engine with a huge boiler and flywheel like the Washington 11 x 17 Duplex Flyer displayed in the Scotia visitors park. In a path like a ski run leading from the engine up to the top of the next mountainside, the trees are sparse, some standing dead with brutally broken trunks, and the ground baked and bare. They ran a high-line operation here, McCollum explains, running logs down from the mountain and up to the road on an overhead cable powered by the steam donkey. It replaced all of the oxen and a lot of the men, and it speeded up the logging process, but it knocked the hell out of everything in the way.

Winding higher, we pass still another kind of forest, logged but left so it's neither jungle nor bare. Instead, above the stumps and healing, steeply sloping land are dozens of tall, skinny redwoods that would look young if the foliage didn't begin so far up the trunk. These are maturing redwoods, one hundred to three hundred years old, long stunted by the shadow of older trees, now left to fatten in sunlight and insure some later logger a living.

With the coming of the "cat," the nearly vertical hill-climbing tractor of the thirties, redwood logging began to change from a skinning operation to a harvesting process. Instead of attacking huge tracts of land with gangs of men, oxen, donkey engines, steam-logging machines and locomotives and cutting everything in reach, the "cat" made it possible to snake out individual logs while leaving neighboring trees intact. For lumber companies with large land holdings, this selective logging meant that a company could, in theory, sustain a regular yield from its existing timberlands indefinitely.

With the help of the forest service and the University of California's School of Forestry, Pacific Lumber began logging selectively before anybody else, and the

112

company is now on a "perpetual sustained-yield basis." Cruising through the woods on foot, a company forester picks out the mature trees and daubs the trees to be cut with white paint, usually amounting to about seventy per cent of a redwood stand. In theory, the remaining trees, maturing faster in the unobstructed light, and seeding new trees in the exposed mineral soil, will keep the company supplied with redwood logs from its own lands in perpetuity. In practice, perpetuity in the red-woods may be as short as twenty years—about as long as Pacific Lumber can expect to be logging virgin growth.

According to William Fischer, formerly chief forester of nearby Six Rivers National Forest, second-growth redwood, one hundred to one hundred and twenty-five years old, doesn't have the growth characteristics or durability of wood from virgin stands. Lumber from the faster-maturing trees doesn't resist disease, insects and decay as well as virgin redwood, and it's not as workable. But neither is—nor does—any other kind of wood.

Since the commercial application of redwood really got underway, about a hundred years ago, the wood's lightness, beauty, strength, nail-holding ability and, above all, its durability have won it the reputation of a superwood. Some virgin redwood timbers, hand-hewn by the Russians for the building of Fort Ross on the California coast near the mouth of the Russian River in the early 1800's, were torn out and brought inland to Sacramento, where they were used in the construction of Sutter's Fort in 1841. They're still there, visibly undeteriorated. For a long time it was a popular western architectural practice to incorporate virgin redwood beams and ties salvaged from railroad trestles and roadbeds into homes and commercial buildings; and the supply gave out a long time before the first beam or tie did. The wood isn't merely rugged, it's superb to handle, with a grain so fine that it was once popularly used to build forms for the casting of metals.

Not even Pacific Lumber's chief forester is making superwood claims for second-growth redwood. But McCollum does insist that, because of selective logging, the company's reserves of original timber are adequate. The company has about forty thousand acres of virgin growth left and is logging at about two thousand acres a year. But there are another fifty thousand acres of residual growth—trees left over from the first go-round—that the company could cut ten years in right now. When the existing virgin stands have been selectively cut in twenty years, there will be a residual base of two billion board feet—according to McCollum, another thirty years.

What seems inevitable in the lumber market is that, as the old-growth redwood forests vanish, the price of virgin redwood lumber will climb to that of mahogany or teak. Already, the redwood firms are moving increasingly toward a plywood-and-pulp economy, and in the planing mill at Scotia, Pacific Lumber has a machine that can brush a laminated plywood panel so that it looks like hand-sawed heart redwood. The Cosmetic Era of American lumbering is almost upon us.

114

As we climb into old growth, the forest begins to shut out the sky, and the land displays the wounds of recent lumbering: fresh-cut stumps, sawdust, exposed mineral soil, sections of trunk, tops of trees.

The land is now so steep on both sides that the road itself seems to be the only spot level enough to stand on. The ground is a mess. It looks as though it has been under an artillery barrage, with craters, gouges, "cat" tracks, branches, stumps and broken-down banks everywhere. If someone were to superimpose a transparency taken at Verdun over a still photograph from a Farm Security Administration Dust-Bowl documentary, it would not present an exaggerated picture of the condition of the soil. All the emotional fuel you'd ever need to fire a conservation drive that would put the redwood industry out of business is right there. It would be so easy. And so unfair. The surrounding chaos, which looks so final, is actually a stage in a cycle. The land heals. It abides. New shoots grow in the exposed soil. And when the siege lifts, reparations are made.

Once, fully half the board-foot mass of the average cut redwood tree was left in the forest, and lost. Some of the trees which, though durable, are extremely sensitive, would shatter upon striking flat ground or grazing a stump; branches, tops and sections of trunk would be left where they lay. Now, firms contract to do clean-up logging, turning what were once forest leftovers into fence posts, shingles, and grape stakes. Drainage ditches and culverts are dug to prevent erosion, and along the banks of creeks and rivers no cutting is allowed at all. Once, redwood forests like these were mined; now they are harvested. And until people are willing, on a private, individual basis, to settle for some lesser material—not just for house siding and beams, but for more personal, visible things like den panelling, a piano, an organ, a casket—then credit must be given to the men who brought about the change.

116

Around a curve at the top of a hill, the road is blocked by a sudden concentration of what seems to be the outsized equipment of a freeway construction crew: a D-8 Cat, a semi and a loader with a claw front. You almost expect to be halted by a flagman with an orange day-glo vest. McCollum pulls the pickup onto the shoulder, stops it at a thirty-degree list, climbs out and starts a low-key conversation with a tall, lean, expressionless man wearing suspenders and a hat turned up all around, reporter-style. Backing and turning, the loader with the claw lifts a forty-foot section of log, pivots, and drops it on the tank-truck-sized bed of the semi, which flinches beneath the weight.

Fully loaded with one redwood log, the semi rumbles off. The road is clear, but rough and loamy; we climb ahead maybe fifty yards, then dive down a steep, fire-trail sort of grade deadending in a deck of large logs.

Beyond, extending out of sight, is a steeply sloping forest of redwoods, with the largest trees averaging over two hundred feet. Fully half have the spike-top of full maturity; they could live another hundred years, but they'd grow no larger.

118

Just beside the road, a driver swings a D-8 Cat back and forth, building a log layout where the next tree will fall. In Mose Sacchi's day, the building of the bed to cushion the impact of the tree was done with picks, shovels, axes and boughs and took the better part of a week. Now the Cat scrapes and grades a level niche out of the hillside in about half an hour.

At the end of the bed, the faller, wearing his aluminum hat at an angle, directs the Cat in shaping the layout, showing the driver where he wants the tree to land. The fallers are the highest paid men in the woods, and the only ones who work on a contract rate, and they exude an obvious confidence in the value of their own effort that makes the general pace of things out here, despite all the equipment, more human than the timed, factory repetitiousness of the mills. They are on top of things, and everything is looser, more relaxed—although the jobs themselves are much more dangerous. There is a fresh presence of risk, a quality of hunch and guess and estimate, of each tree being different, and of being out on the edge of whatever it is that all civilized men are a part of, that seems to give men in the woods a quiet sense of independence that fits them like old clothes.

123

The faller and his brother, both dressed in hickory shirt and Levis, work as a team, falling each tree and bucking it into truck-length logs. As the Cat driver completes the layout, the brothers are already methodically at work on the cut. Standing on two-by-fours resting on drivers—wedges driven into the trunk just above the tree's butt—holding a snarling, smoking chain saw with a five-foot bar, the boss brother, the chopper, cuts a mouth-like opening in the side facing the direction they want the tree to fall—the undercut. Without it, the bar of the saw would be pinched by the tree's weight, and even if you could somehow cut on through the tree's seven-foot diameter, without the undercut there would be no way to control the direction of its fall, a fall that is so crucial that it isn't rain, but wind, that can shut a woods crew down for a day.

125

The undercut completed, the chopper now moves his saw around and starts in from the other side. All the machinery but the saw has stopped; gradually, the men begin giving way, walking back out of the path of the two-hundred-and-fifty-foot tree. There is sawdust everywhere and smoke like sweat from the saw's dogged straining. Then quiet. The cut is finished.

"Heyyy-up-up-up!" the chopper calls; the tree is falling, up the hill.

There are a couple of resounding beats, like taps on a large drum, then a profound, thunderous crack, the wood-on-wood sound of branches breaking and a huge rush of foliage as the tree sweeps across the sky like a needle falling in a gauge, landing out of sight with a thump that the earth transmits to the base of your spinal column.

Suddenly, the sky seems empty and the ground full.

128

There is a strange rush of feeling, half remorse and half—let us confess—satisfaction at seeing something living outside time reduced to human mortality.

Before the dust settles, the fallers are walking the log in their calk books, measuring the board feet by which they're paid. The bucker's first section cut is eighty-three inches—an inch short of seven feet thick—and the section figures out at about two thousand board feet. All together, the tree is estimated at about twelve or thirteen thousand, or enough lumber to build two houses. An average-size redwood, according to McCollum.

Standing between two spicy-smelling sections of the log, you are in wood over your head, inside the soft bark and white sapwood, staring at the scars of centuries-old fires and drought, adding up more than five hundred years in rings, watching the tree grow darker, richer, redder as it gets to its beautiful, dead heart.

133

Back in the truck, McCollum calls in over a hissing, cab-style radio, telling a voice at Scotia where he is and where we're heading, as through the side windows, the woods, which are just a fraction of his responsibility, thin and then thicken as the era of their logging recedes. He begins to talk about his job, and some of the adopted tour-guide country manner begins to peel away. McCollum is an intelligent man with perhaps the company's most difficult administrative job, a graduate of Berkeley with a son who'll be starting at Uppsala in Sweden in a month. He is out here not because the company can spare him, but because Pacific Lumber is traditionally lean on the management side, and the woods are his.

He is aware of the explosions in the world that are sending ripples of change out here in the woods. Strange people now move into the company lands, not to hunt or poach timber, but to live. In an attempt to ease the pressure of conservation demands, hundreds of company acres are now opened by permit on weekends—an administrative nuisance, and a necessity. Without the permits, there is the possibility that Pacific Lumber, by allowing people to roam its timberlands unrestricted, would lose its proscriptive rights, and the land would become a park. There are requests for campgrounds, sewage, water and garbage facilities, but how the company could provide them, McCollum does not know. Most disturbing of all is the urban-guerrilla vandalism that seems to have moved out into the wilderness. On one weekend a Diesel-fuel storage tank, miles from the nearest paved road, was opened and left to drain out over the ground. "They didn't even steal it," says McCollum, uncomprehending, "just opened it up and let it run out." On another weekend a group of people defecated on the seat and controls of a tractor. McCollum recounts these incidents in the disillusioned tone of the propertied man who has come to the familiar pessimistic conclusions about "human nature." The company has land. People want land. And from the millennium there is no isolation.

135

Coming out of the company lands, we pass through a gate and, by way of a county road, arrive back at the highway. Heading north through gray, marshy, river-mouth country overhung with coastal fog, we turn off at Freshwater, the company's old port of embarkation, and climb again into timber.

Alongside the road is a stand of mature second-growth redwood, sprung from lands logged out over a hundred years ago. The new growth is so thick that the forest is impossible to see into beyond a few yards, and there is an almost unnatural symmetry to the trees, which all seem to be the same height and thickness. The overall effect is one of tidiness and predictability, as if someone had deliberately grown a woods as a movie set for a live-action version of Hansel and Gretel.

Continuing along the road toward what McCollum promises will be a full-scale second-growth logging operation, we take a dirt turnoff into Pacific Lumber land, and accidentally catch two trespassers in the act.

About fifty feet in from the pavement, two young men about eighteen or nineteen stand in a strip of company road, a break in the trees dotted with bits of broken glass, tires and garbage. One of them is holding a .22 rifle and both conspicuously avoid looking at the orange and green company truck as it pulls up beside their car.

"Watch this," says McCollum, swinging out of the truck to talk to them. The identification with the boys outside the truck, caught, trying to be cool, is total. Old questions ring in the ears: "Okay, where'd you buy the beer?" But McCollum handles the situation surprisingly well. He is firm, but not belligerent or recriminatory. The boys are polite, somewhat shamefaced, and quietly plead their ignorance of trespassing on anybody's private land. Indeed, from the look of the land around them, with bits of broken bottles and tin cans on the ground, on logs and boxes, and a bullet-riddled automobile hulk in an adjoining gulch, this spot of land is a *de facto* local rifle range, with prohibitory notices no one can enforce. The boys' crime is not trespassing, but getting caught, and both they and McCollum know it. He will give a brief lecture and, appropriately contrite, they will listen, and nothing more will come of it. Which is exactly what happens. In the end, he offers the boys a permit to use the woods on weekends; all they have to do is stop by the office anytime and pick it up. With surprising dignity, both boys refuse. They'll go shoot somewhere else. McCollum repeats the offer, and again the boys refuse. At last, he lets them go, and, still polite, they get into their car and back it on out to the highway. When McCollum returns to the truck, he has been put a bit off-balance by their refusal.

"It can get very touchy out here. You can't arrest people, only warn them. You start getting high-handed, and first thing you know, somebody comes back and sets the woods on fire."

Later, back down near the main highway, McCollum attempts to explain himself in terms of the frustrations of his job, trying to show what it is like to try and live and work rationally in the emotional atmosphere engendered by the redwoods and to be charged with imposing order on a wilderness. Pulling the truck over to the side of the road, he points to a thinned stand of trees on the edge of the company's property, bordering a lot with a private home.

"You see that stand of timber there? I told the man who lives in that house, 'I'm going to do you a favor. We're going to cut three-quarters of an acre near the road. We'll hardly touch the forest, increase visibility, and clear up all the slash.' Which is what we did. So a man who lives across the road writes a letter to the president of the company, accusing Pacific Lumber of laying waste the redwoods. The man who wrote the letter is an engineer and *he* works for one of the companies that clear-cuts."

the
company

As if in an earthquake, the corrugated walls and wooden floor of the old upstairs office shudder, and everything within—technical manuals, papers, coffee cups, furniture, people—vibrates with the heavy, rolling transmitted shock of the machinery of the mill. Behind a desk, Machine Superintendent Don Thompson sits with his hat on, pausing on his daily round of looking after the mill works that now almost drown his voice. Looking around, it seems amazing that the office with its lath trim and high ceiling suggesting a small-town railroad depot has survived decades of this palsied trembling. Yet the big clock not only remains on the wall, it ticks steadily and keeps good time; the weighted papers remain on the desk; and Thompson manages to make himself heard without violating his even country manner.

The noise and the trembling are things Thompson has gradually learned to live with, like the swollen responsibilities of his job. A man who began with Pacific Lumber as a blacksmith's helper in a logging camp, Thompson is now in charge of the repair of rolling stock, doctoring failures and performing maintenance on all the production lines, servicing the power-system boilers that run twenty-four hours a day, and caring for the sensitive chain and drive mechanism of the debarker. When the company built its own plywood plant, it was Thompson who helped set up the design.

"People grow up with this place," says Don Thompson. "And a lot of the things about it are in their heads. For instance, so much of the mill machinery was made so long ago that we have to make our own parts for a lot of things. And our construction millwrights can do anything from digging a ditch to building a sawmill. We generate all our own electricity, including power for the town. It would be cheaper if we didn't now, but it's too costly to change over."

Thompson, who lived in Scotia as long ago as 1913 and has moved back to the town several times since, now owns a twenty-acre ranch at Shively, about two or three miles up the Eel River. His house is on a knoll at the crest of a quarter-mile slope of field that ends in a bluff above the river. From the knoll, standing at eye level with the green superstructure girders of a nearby highway bridge, it seems inconceivable that the river could ever spread over the bluff, come all the way up the slope and send currents rushing through the house. And so it seemed to Thompson and his wife until December of 1964.

For weeks rain had been falling on the island communities as it usually falls out where the mountains bunch up beside the Pacific: a continuous drizzle, with great surf-like waves of drenching cloudburst. Toward Christmas, the Eel River ballooned to the full superhighway width of its bed and, the lands around it saturated, began oozing into the low-lying areas beyond. At Pepperwood, where the Eel had taken away whole houses in 1955, people were being evacuated again with their belongings. Over the undrained lands around the river, sirens were whooping throughout the night, asking for and announcing help.

At their ranch, Thompson and his wife, figuring that the 1955 flood—the worst in local history—hadn't reached them, decided they would wait the river out. It *had* to stop raining sometime and, judging from the radio reports, there didn't seem any better places to be.

On December 22 the water rose above the Northwestern Pacific tracks and trestles along the Scotia Bluffs, and the schools in Rio Dell were closed. At Scotia, Pacific Lumber had evacuated twelve families from the houses along Railroad Avenue, as the water rose over the tracks and entered the depot; there was fear that the company's cold deck, an enormous stack of unprocessed logs stored at the Scotia park, would break loose and be carried away by the river, where the logs would batter everything in the water's path.

After the water broke over the bank, it began to rise quickly over the Thompsons' ranch land; soon the house was isolated, the knoll an island, and still the rain was falling. This was not to be simply 1955 again. Like thousands of other people throughout northwestern California, the Thompsons began to realize that they were inhabiting an event beyond all previous catastrophe and that at the edges of their moderated lives ancient extremities—suffering, death, financial ruin—were beginning to appear. The bill for dwelling close to nature was falling due.

At Scotia, logs from the cold deck began breaking loose and drifting out into the current, joining other logs carried from upriver; small jams formed and broke apart; torpedo-like, seventy-ton logs were slamming downriver toward the bridges below; those that struck the piers made the roadbeds swerve and shook the super-structures. First outbuildings, sheds and shacks, then whole houses floated by on the boiling, brown, log-strewn waters. The bridges were closed to traffic, and the highway patrol began to push back sightseers.

By three o'clock the Thompsons' phone and electricity had gone out. Some of their cattle were bellowing for help, others swimming toward the barn, bumping into cars and farm machinery. Their house itself no longer safe, the Thompsons were alone and without higher ground, surrounded by the mad rush of the river.

At five o'clock the Thompsons left their house and, carrying a Coleman lantern and a few leftovers from the kitchen, sloshed on planks across their front yard and climbed up the water tower, a wooden tank and platform set on top of an ancient, burned-out redwood stump.

Earlier that day, Don Thompson had nailed a sheet of canvas under the eaves of the tank-top as a makeshift shelter, just in case. Now he and his wife huddled inside the canvas, out of the worst of the rain, and waited for whatever was to come to them and their ranch.

By nightfall, the water had entered the house and was running over the floors. Outside, Thompson's new 1964 Mercury sagged on its springs, waterlogged. Around them the Thompsons' ranch land had disappeared under a vast, moving lake, laden with logs, trees, houses and other huge debris that made the big stump and the water tower quiver as they struck it. First with a pole, and then with his foot, Thompson pushed tree limbs away from the tower to keep a jam from forming that would tear the tower from its moorings.

All night the Thompsons clung to their buoy on a new inland sea, watching a lightless horizon under a starless sky, where the water was the beginning and end of everything and the air was alive with terror. From the ranch next door came the scream of a horse, trapped and drowning; and from below, the last, horrified cries of their own doomed cattle, all lost in the endless, onward gush of rain and river. In the morning, the water had risen to the middle of the windows of the Thompsons' house. Cattle, cars, farm machinery—all were gone. The rain had slackened, and there were openings here and there in the sky, but to the east, the river still looked a full mile wide.

Later that day, the Thompsons were evacuated by boat to Scotia, where they found the familiar community with an odd, truncated look: the entire lower part of the town—about twenty houses, the ball park, sewage plant, pumping plant, train depot, and the cold deck—was gone. Only the old slaughterhouse, built on a rise, remained, breasting the moving water like a steaming ship.

The residential streets, which had always had a certain army-post tidiness, now seemed fully militarized, with relief helicopters, one after another, hanging in the sky, then falling softly to the street in front of the main office, to deliver medicine, milk and food. This militaryness of things carried over into the lives of the people who now endured a war-zone lack of comforts as basic as dry clothing or heat. (You got damp and you stayed damp.) And who began to display a certain classic camaraderie of hardship. In a community of dedicated hunters and campers, there were plenty of lanterns, cookstoves and heaters available to be loaned out, while in a resurgence of frontier hospitality some people, like the friends who took in the Thompsons, vacated their beds and moved to couches for the duration.

For Pacific Lumber, the flood and the weeks of emergency that followed represented an attack on the whole concept of the town, the company, and the possibilities of a moderated life. Unruly nature, subdued and forgotten in the quiet streets

145

of the town and the niceness of local life, had slipped the traces and trampled the charioteer.

Close to eighteen million feet of redwood logs had been lost, and countless stacks of even more valuable seasoned lumber. A whole street of houses was destroyed, leaving nearly two dozen families homeless. Water had run through the factory to a depth of five feet, and had risen even higher in the sheds and buildings nearer to the river. Electric motors, blades and precision tools were ruined. As a precautionary measure, the steam from the boilers had been released, and for a time the town was without electricity or heat. In the woods, roads and bridges were out, and logging equipment stranded. Even if the mills had been able to resume operating, there was no way to ship lumber. Bridges both north and south of town had been amputated by the river, and the Northwestern Pacific had lost more than a hundred miles of track. It would be months before normal transportation could be restored. Unlike more diversified corporations, Pacific Lumber could not simply shift the burden of its operation to another plant in a distant city and continue filling orders. With mills, factory and yards all concentrated at Scotia, and Scotia isolated, the company was, at least temporarily, out of business. Within the paternalistic society of the community itself, the outlook could hardly be worse. Father was out of work, with everyone depending on him.

Beneath the calm surface of local life, awful rocks and chasms had appeared, and for some people the security of Scotia had vanished, an illusion. Rather than face the massive ordeal of cleaning up the piles of scattered logs and lumber and foul-smelling river silt, of drying out mattresses and throwing away rugs, of picking

146

up your whole life and shaking it out only to settle back in the same vulnerable spot, quite a few people just let everything go and quit the area completely, deserting land and abandoning furniture. One family, stranded out of town for days, was finally returned to Scotia by a rescue team; on arriving back at their company house, they simply packed their belongings, left without saying goodbye, and moved to Arkansas.

In southern Humboldt County it had always seemed that, whatever happened, the company somehow must have a hand in it. Now, some people, ignoring the record rainfall, adopted the view that the company's logging operations had so eroded the local watershed over the years that Pacific Lumber was, in fact, responsible for the flood. Reflected in the risen river waters, the image of the company itself seemed muddied.

In the near-desperate circumstances of what seemed to be its appointed hour, the managment of Pacific Lumber set and stuck to a simple, eloquent priority: people first. And assumed its old role as sole provider for a complex and remote community. While the town and plant were still disabled, while retrievable logs littered the flood plain and salvageable equipment rusted and mildewed, Pacific Lumber trucks went out with blankets, food and fuel to people who could survive where they were, and brought in, clothed and housed the people who had to be evacuated. The plywood plant was transformed into a gigantic dormitory and furniture warehouse. Company crews were put to work repairing the bridges and roads. Tons of crushed rock from the maintenance yards were poured into washes along Highway 101. Part of the Scotia water supply was diverted across the river, where it served the town of Rio Dell for more than six months. The drying kilns were fired up, not to salvage retrieved lumber, but to dry mattresses and furniture.

The help that was given was personal and individual, a simple redistribution of burdens among fellow victims, based on need and on what could be spared. Both Pacific Lumber and the Salvation Army—the first relief organization into the flood lands—gave what was needed openly and without asking questions. Only later, when other relief organizations moved in with complex priorities and bureaucratic procedures, did an ugly grabbiness and competition arise among some of the survivors. According to Martin Marks, who kept track of what Pacific Lumber spent on direct flood relief in hope of some sort of reimbursement, Federal Disaster Funds covered only about a third of it.

Out of the flood and the company's response to it came a new sense of communion and intimacy, a confidence born of an individual's sense of his own luck and hardiness, and of shared hardship and overall company concern.

"In a way it was the best time we ever had here," one man who has lived more than fifty years in the area admits rather wistfully. "I don't think people have ever felt so close."

When Don Thompson, driving a loaned company car, returned to his ranch early in January, the ground was covered with a layer of river silt so soft that the Army Corps of Engineers, cleaning up the dead cattle and rebuilding the river bank, couldn't drive their tractors on it. Instead, getting permission from Thompson to cross corners of his land, they promised they'd come back. But never did. Thompson's house, whose mortgage had been all but paid off, still stood, but six feet of water had run through it and had ruined practically everything inside. Outside, the yard

148

was a mass of evil-smelling silt, waterlogged cars and farm machinery, splintered driftwood and pathetic Christmas decorations.

Today, more than six years later, the Thompsons' property still bears the scars and stains of high water. Inside the house, there are no carpets on the floors, and you can still detect a dank, basement smell; outside, a walk of planks leads across the lawn, as though another rain-swept dash to the water tower were anticipated momentarily. Beyond the tower, the slope going down the river is oddly bare of trees.

Behind the ranch, the State Division of Highways has built a huge, crushed-rock dike, part of a new stretch of freeway scheduled for completion in two more years that will expose the Thompsons' property still more to flooding. As part of the same freeway project, the state has cut a drainage ditch across Thompson's ranch which almost completely devalues his property, and for which the Highway men have offered to reimburse Thompson less than two thousand dollars.

"I didn't expect the state to be like that," says Thompson bitterly. "When they came in, all they said was, 'This is what we're going to take, and this is what we're going to give you for it,' and they kept repeating it whenever they said anything. I guess I wasn't used to anything like that, working for the company. They don't treat people that way."

Sitting in his office in the mill in the company town, pondering the vicissitudes of land ownership, and the private dealings of public bodies, reflecting on the contrast between the way the outside world treats people when they are down and the way Pacific Lumber, stunned by flood, responded to people when it was down, Don Thompson says that if he could sell his ranch, he'd move back into Scotia.

"We're a paternalistic company," says Stanwood Murphy, president of Pacific Lumber. "I know that's a dirty word, but it's accurate."

Slouching informally in his presidential chair, his large hands miniaturizing the coffee mug on his desk, Murphy, a tall, thickly built, big-featured man with disappearing red hair and a deep voice, looks more like the logger of folklore than most of the men who work on his crews out in the woods.

His office, dark, redwood-panelled, in a ground-floor corner of the administration building, has both the size and spongy quiet of a large suburban living room. Through the venetian blinds is a midtown block of Scotia's Main Street, bathed in soft light, the flagpole icy white, surrounded by trim green lawn, the museum and visitors park being tidied up by a garden crew, the directors cottage under large, old shade trees, framed by three windows like a New England triptych hanging from a California sky. Only the mills, stretching off behind the other side of this building, seem oddly out of sight. In the room's insulated comfort, you don't even hear their noise.

Sitting in his office in a town where his firm owns all the land and all the buildings, surrounded by tens of thousands of acres of company timberlands, Stanwood Murphy inhabits a situation more like that of a medieval feudal baron than anything in contemporary America. When he speaks, it is with the candor of a man who is accustomed to saying what he thinks. For all the slouching informality, it isn't hard to imagine him bellowing somebody out of a room.

"We lose money on the town," he admits. "Not as much as we lose on the hotel and restaurant, but some. We figure it's worth it, to keep a good crew on here."

A few years back, according to Murphy, a Southern California land-development firm was interested in acquiring Scotia as a real estate venture. "They specialized in the field and had developed McCloud, which had been a company

town. They do a good job, but we weren't interested. We have no intention of selling Scotia."

Pacific Lumber is now the last major independent lumber company left in the redwoods. In an era of mergers and acquisitions, the company, with its enormous landholdings and lean management, would seem to be attractive game for some stalking conglomerate.

Murphy smiles, recognizing a familiar problem. "We know we've been eyed by the raiders. About two years ago, we had a lot of cash, and we had to fight off an outside raid." To make the prey a little harder to swallow, Pacific Lumber diversified itself, using the money to acquire a brush manufacturing firm, a company that makes welding equipment, and nearly five thousand acres of Sacramento Valley farmland. Murphy thinks the era of corporate raiding is just about over, but he knocks on his desk when he says it.

The cash that Murphy refers to was payment, made by the State of California, for the Avenue of the Giants, the tunnel of magnificent redwoods a few miles south of the town. According to retired Federal Forester William Fischer, Pacific Lumber, "the most public-minded company in the redwoods," pledged the stand of trees to the state in the 1920's, then had to pay taxes on it for more than forty years until the Assembly appropriated the funds to buy it.

"We used to have a pretty good case when people would come in here and get sore at us for cutting trees," says Murphy. "We could just point to the Avenue of the Giants. Now we can't do that anymore."

Murphy is sensitive to the pressure for public parks, forests and recreation land in the redwoods that seems certain to increase during the seventies. During the dispute over Redwood National Park, a proposed combination of transferred State Park forest lands and private timberlands set aside by the Federal Government, which was to include some thirty thousand acres of lumber-company owned lands, one of the other redwood companies began "spite logging"—deliberately cutting lands designated for the park. At the time, Murphy prevailed on the company's management to stop cutting the proscribed trees until he was bluntly told to keep his nose out of his competitor's business.

When the park was finally dedicated in 1968, and it turned out that the company whose logging practices had been the most offensive was required to cede the largest share of private timber acreage, it wasn't only people outside the lumber industry who felt that a certain justice had been served.

Studying Murphy's informal manner, listening to his direct speech, you begin to sense the man's pride at having transcended the iron determinism of his situation. Born into an almost monarchial family, aware from the days when his mother used to lead the Murphy children around the company lands on a pony that he was heir to a timber patriarchate, Murphy has somehow acquired the unsentimental compassion and commanding physical presence of a self-made man. Somewhere along the way, he has been tempered. Gradually, the unavoidable parallel begins to make itself felt: the enormous wealth, the secluded estate, the Irish name; there was even a brother who suffered an untimely death.

Looking up into the face of A. S. Murphy staring from his son's office wall, the parallel is suddenly complete. In the photograph, probably taken during the thirties, Murphy's father—stiffly posed, hair prematurely white, wearing round-lensed horn-rimmed glasses—is a ringer for Joseph P. Kennedy.

At ten minutes past four, in the steamfitters room in Mill B, underneath the huge electric-generating turbines, Harry Scholl's retirement party is just getting underway. In the bright fluorescent light of the room, there's an urn of coffee today and some cups brought down from the hotel kitchen and a large cake in a pan. Some of the men who work with Harry are there, nibbling cake and sipping coffee, and after awhile Ed Carpenter, Scotia's resident manager, comes down from the main office along with Martin Marks and Gary Cook from Personnel. From time to time, old friends drop in, to shyly wish Harry goodbye or stand around and talk awhile. Carpenter, who doesn't look it, tells Harry he's sixty years old and hopes to do as well as Harry when he retires. Harry, a taciturn man with the pressed lips of a person on intimate terms with pain, listens uneasily as the men from the office and the men from the mill exchange the bits of local history that seem to be the strongest bond between them.

"Remember when the old bunkhouse was up there?"

"Yeah, and I was working on the Green Chain?"

There seems to be great reverence, if not for the man, then for the moment, as though, amid the conversational groping, the true significance of staying on with Pacific Lumber twenty, thirty or forty years were about to be revealed; as if it all should come together here, the town, the company, the mills, the woods, and take on some higher meaning.

"Harry's the best boiler tender we ever had," one of his buddies tells you. "We'll miss him."

"You've done it better than I could," says Ed Carpenter, with unintentional irony.

It's an open and gregarious party, although there is no booze. Company rules prohibit drinking on the job, though when a man from the main office retires, the party sometimes moves on to a dinner and drinking in a backroom of the Scotia Inn.

Corky Kemp comes by, looking a little weary, perhaps thinking of the forty-one years he has to go before his own retirement party. And Fred Elliott's father, Ted, pops in the door, bolts a cup of coffee and leaves, perhaps deferring the moment for *his* retirement, a little more than a month away.

After a while, as the party settles into a dozen small conversations, it's possible to talk to Harry Scholl a little about himself.

"I raised five kids," he tells you. "Used to live in Scotia." In 1924, Harry Scholl was fired by the Pacific Lumber Company for taking a battery charger from the monorail shed, installing it in the bunkhouse where he was sleeping, and using it to run a crystal set. A company inspection, pulled periodically in those days, caught Harry with a 300-watt bulb from the monorail shed as well.

It was a flick of the whip. A tug on the company reins.

Later, Harry was hired back as a crane operator. Got married, settled down, and began minding the steam turbines that generate electricity for the mills and the town. For the past thirty years, his working life has consisted of sitting around at odd hours, taking occasional water samples from the turbines, and testing them. Now that's over, and Harry says he'll fish and do scrimshaw with redwood burls. He says he's always had odd-hour shifts, so he won't be bolting out of bed every morning to get to PL. "But I'll have to stay up all night every now and again and pretend I'm pulling a graveyard."

Watching Harry Scholl, as he steals a solitary look at the fishing rod and reel the boys have chipped in to buy him, the symbol of both his thirty years on the job and his future away from it, you can't help wondering, with Harry, what the sum of it all really is, if "staying on" amounts to anything more than a fishing rod, some coffee and cake, social security and a pension.

Then, while he's still admiring his new fishing rod with its good reel, Harry gets a telephone call on the company line, from his daughter who lives in Tennessee, and you can tell from the look on his face and the light in his eyes that it's the one thing that happened today that's made him truly happy.

158

While Harry is talking to his daughter, a steamfitter points out a group of three poplar trees, planted outside the door, two years ago, right next to the log pond.

"They grow fast," he says. "In just a year—you see that brace running along the conveyor belt? Well, they were below that in the spring. Now they're way above it."

The steamfitter can see the trees from the window in the door of the shack. Next to the door is the water bubbler, and next to that the sink where he washes his hands each night before he goes home. And every night as he's washing up, consciously or subconsciously, he will check those trees to see if they're all right. He will want to know. Right now, they're changing color. And someday, if he raises his eyes just a bit, he'll see trees in the midst of all the cast iron he handles every day. Thick and leafy. Trees that he and another man planted. And that will be fine with the company, because any way a man can make his job more personal means it's more likely that he's going to be staying on.

And, should the steamfitter see those same trees grow to be fifty or a hundred feet tall, stretching out until they look like they have been on that spot forever, older than the pond or the town or the mills, old like the redwoods, he may, someday, take his last look at them from a party like this one, surrounded by friends, and men he's worked with, and brass down from the main office, sipping company coffee and eating company cake, waiting for the last whistle on his last working day in one of the last company towns in America.